HISTORY IN PICTURES

World War One
THE GREAT BATTLES

Robert Hamilton

Trans
Atlantic
Press

Germany invades Belgium

Germany declared war on Russia on August 1, 1914 and immediately instigated the Schlieffen Plan; a rapid strike towards Paris to neutralize the inevitable threat from France, which was to be followed by an attack on Russia. The German army stormed through Belgium and Liege, the fortress town, fell. Belgium immediately appealed to Britain for help. Asquith issued an ultimatum but with no response coming from the German chancellor, Theobald Bethmann-Hollweg, Britain declared war on Germany on August 5. By now German troops were advancing through Belgium and the country's government left Brussels for Antwerp on August 17. Only three days later Belgium's capital was in German hands.

The Battle of the Marne

Germany's initial success disguised several major weaknesses; the army was overstretched and undersupplied. The Russians went on the offensive in August and two corps were redeployed east, just as the British Expeditionary Force began arriving to shore up French defences. Nevertheless, the Germans were within striking distance of Paris and the Allies had to act quickly to save the French capital. The result was the Battle of the Marne, which took place in early September 1914. A great number of men were killed on both sides, but the battle resulted in a German retreat. The Germans moved to a more easily defendable position on the high ground north of the Aisne river. Neither side could make further headway and a long war of attrition set in.

BELOW: Fallen soldiers strew the ground following the Battle of the Marne.

OPPOSITE: The remnants of the Russian Second Army in full-scale retreat after the crushing defeat at the Battle of Tannenberg.

The Battle of Tannenburg

The Schlieffen Plan meant that Germany only allocated minimal resources to the Russian Front in 1914. Germany's Eighth Army, under the command of General Prittwitz, was sent to the east to hold the line while war was waged against France in the west. The Russian army was inferior to the Germans in terms of training and leadership, but vastly superior in terms of numbers. This caused Prittwitz to panic and order a partial retreat, so an angry government in Berlin replaced him with generals Hindenberg and Ludendorff.

In August 1914, the Russian generals planned to strike at the Eighth Army, which was based to the west of the Masurian Lakes. The Russian First Army would go around the lakes to the north and the Second Army would do so from the south in order to trap the Germans in a classic pincer movement. However, things did not go according to plan because the Germans intercepted radio communication between the two armies. Knowing his troops were no match for both Russian armies, General Hindenberg marched to engage the Second Army while the First was too far away. The resulting battle near Tannenberg was a disaster for Russia; the Second Army was almost wiped out, 30,000 men were killed and 100,000 were taken prisoner.

The Battle of the Masurian Lakes

Hindenberg and Ludendorff then turned their attention to the First Army, commanded by General Rennenkampf. The Battle of the Masurian Lakes began on September 9, 1914. The battle was not quite the disaster for the Russians that Tannenberg had been, but the First Army only escaped to fight another day because of Rennenkampf's decision to retreat.

To capitalize on Germany's successes, Austria-Hungary began an offensive in Galicia in September, but the ramshackle imperial army was unable to defeat the Russians who took the strategic fortress of Lemberg. Germany's new Chief of Staff, Erich von Falkenhayn, wanted to turn its attention back to the Western Front, but he had to reinforce Austria-Hungary in the east. As a result, a major redeployment of troops from the west to the east took place.

The Battle of Neuve Chapelle

On March 10, the Allies made their first serious attempt to break through the enemy line at the village of Neuve Chapelle. The settlement itself was successfully seized from German hands, although Sir John French's report on the battle was grim (and a foretaste of worse to come): there had been a gain of some three hundred yards on a front just half a mile in length – but it had cost the Allies 12,000 men either killed, wounded or missing.

The Battle of Neuve Chapelle was the first planned British offensive of the war.

OPPOSITE BELOW: Russian soldiers creep across no man's land to cut wires in front of German Trenches. Trench warfare was rare in the east because the front was so long.

OPPOSITE ABOVE: Downtime in the Russian ranks from the gruelling fighting on the Eastern Front.

RIGHT: Although, they managed to capture the village of Neuve Chapelle itself, the offensive was eventually abandoned after the British registered severe losses.

ABOVE: The 12,000 casualties at Neuve Chapelle were a foretaste of the worse to come.

War in the air

The First World War witnessed the birth of aviation in warfare. Both sides had to contend with this new front and develop this new technology for use in war. German Zeppelins had bombed Paris at the start of the conflict, and the British had to face an aerial bombardment for the first time on January 19, 1915. Parts of the Norfolk coastline came under attack, and this was followed by raids on the south-east and the North Sea coast over the next few months. There were not many fatalities, but they were almost all civilians. The targeted killing of non-combatants in this way added a new dimension to the war, which was termed 'frightfulness' at the time. By employing this new tactic, the Central Powers hoped to damage morale rather than inflict huge casualties, and they soon extended it to the oceans as well.

BELOW: Bomb damage from a Zeppelin raid on Bury St Edmunds, England

OPPOSITE: The British fleet, viewed from the deck of HMS *Audacious*. This was the first major British battleship lost in the war when it hit a mine off the coast of Ireland in October 1914.

OPPOSITE INSET: The sinking of the Kaiser's battleship, *Blücher*, at Dogger Bank in 1915. The crew scrambles along her plates in an attempt to abandon ship.

War in the sea

Germany declared the waters around Britain and Ireland to be a war region in February 1915 and began a blockade of the seas around the British Isles using submarines and mines. However, the war at sea was, for the most part, a stalemate because neither side was keen to engage the other. The Allies feared German U-Boats and the Germans feared British naval superiority. To try to break the deadlock, the Germans announced that commercial shipping would now be attacked without any warning. This caused outrage and Winston Churchill, then First Lord of the Admiralty, condemned it as 'open piracy and murder on the high seas' when he spoke in the House of Commons.

Sinking of the *Lusitania*

The threat became reality on May 7, in a way which had profound ramifications. Over 1,000 people died when the Cunard liner *Lusitania* was sunk a few miles off the Irish coast. A week before, the German embassy in the United States had issued a statement announcing that the *Lusitania* was a potential target, but only a few among the many passengers took the threat seriously enough to cancel their voyage. The loss of 128 American lives generated a strong tide of anti-German feeling in the States and was actually the first step towards American involvement in the war. These same feelings of shock and disgust were also widespread in Britain, where anti-German sentiment rose sharply and violently. This change in the public mood led the Royal Family to change its name from the House of Saxe-Coburg to the House of Windsor.

Gallipoli

At the outbreak of war, it had been thought that the Allies' naval strength would turn out to be a vital factor. The first six months of the conflict had shown little evidence of this, but in early 1915 an Anglo–French task force was deployed in the Mediterranean with the aim of changing the situation. The plan was to attack Turkey, which had joined the Central Powers in 1914, through the straits of the Dardanelles – the narrow waterway from the Aegean Sea which led all the way to Constantinople. If the Allies could take Constantinople, then there was every chance that they would be able to win a passage through to their Russian allies.

Accordingly, in February 1915 the forts at the entrance to the Dardanelles were bombarded by a fleet led by Vice-Admiral Sackville Carden. However, progress up the straits was slow and three battleships were lost to mines on March 18. As a result, it was decided that the eventual success of the Dardanelles campaign would depend on the deployment of land forces, an obvious decision in the circumstances and one which came as no surprise whatsoever to the Turks.

The landings

On April 25, some British and French troops, together with soldiers from the Australian and New Zealand Army Corps (ANZAC), landed on the Gallipoli Peninsula. Turkish soldiers had been expecting the landings and were lying in wait in strong fortifications above the beaches. British and French troops landing at Cape Helles on the tip of the peninsula came under severe fire and barely managed to capture the beach. At the end of the first day their forces were too depleted to mount an advance beyond the beach.

To the north, ANZAC troops faced an even worse situation. They landed almost a mile off course and faced an impossible terrain. Trapped between the sea and the surrounding hills, they were lambs to the slaughter.

ABOVE: Australian troops on the way to Gallipoli. The boats carrying Australian and New Zealander servicemen drifted off course and the men went ashore at the wrong beach.

OPPOSITE: Troops aboard SS *Nile*, prepare to land on the Gallipoli Peninsula.

DAILY MAIL   DECEMBER 14, 1914

The Dardanelles

The Dardanelles (the ancient Hellespont) is a narrow channel separating Europe from Asia and connecting the Sea of Marmara and the Aegean Sea. It is about 40 miles long. The shores at the mouth are about two miles apart, but the waterway then widens considerably, gradually to contract again until it reaches 'the Narrows' eleven miles up, where it is less than a mile wide. There are two sets of defences, one at the mouth and the other at the Narrows. During the war with Italy it was stated that the Turks arranged a minefield below the Narrows.

The passage of the straits was forced by the British squadron under Sir John Duckworth in February 1807, but he repassed them with great loss in March, the castles of Seston and Abydos hurling down stone shot upon the British ships. The British Mediterranean Fleet also unceremoniously steamed through the Hellespont in 1878.

Failure at Gallipoli

With the Allies pinned down, a fresh landing at the parched Suvla Bay was carried out in August but it came to nothing, and did so quickly. Casualties, both from enemy action and disease, were dreadful. Churchill, who had been one of the chief advocates of the Dardanelles campaign, had spoken of being just 'a few miles from victory', but by November 1915 it was clear that there were no options left: retreat was the only possibility. Sir Charles Munro replaced Hamilton, and was charged with leading the evacuation. Churchill resigned. The withdrawal from the straits, at least, was a spectacular success. It took place between December and January in almost total secrecy. The entire campaign cost the Allies more than 250,000 men.

BELOW: Going over the top at Gallipoli. The Dardanelles campaign quickly succumbed to the deadlock and heavy losses the Allies had been experiencing on the Western Front.

LEFT: Members of the Australian Imperial Guards listen to music with the enemy less than 30 yards away.

OPPOSITE: British and French troops come ashore at Cape Helles on the Gallipoli Peninsula.

Daily Mail   December 21, 1915

Undoing the Dardanelles blunder

The withdrawal of the British troops from two of the three points held on the Gallipoli Peninsula may be taken as a sign that the Government has at last realized the stupendous blunder it committed in venturing upon this expedition, the earlier phases of which Mr. Churchill described as a 'gamble'. A gamble it has proved in the lives of the most heroic of our race. The casualties at the Dardanelles numbered up to November 9 no fewer than 106,000 officers and men. In addition, sickness on this front accounted for 90,000 down to October. A loss of nearly 200,000 men was thus incurred without any adequate result.

Not only did the Government despatch to the Dardanelles forces which, judiciously utilized at other points, might have achieved the greatest results; not only did it divert to the Near East munitions at a time when we were perilously short of high-explosive shells, it also deceived the nation as to the position and prospects after its strokes had signally failed through initial mismanagement or the inadequacy of the army employed. The public has not forgotten the optimistic assurances of Mr. Churchill, Lord Robert Cecil, and Lord Kitchener.

Mr. Lloyd George's speech last evening really contains the gravest indictment that has as yet been drawn against the Government. Here is a confession that when the Germans were in May making 250,000 high-explosive shells a day the British production was only 2,500. Even now he implies that, despite great efforts, we have not equalled the German output. Shall we ever overtake it? Only if the nation works its hardest. The fatal words of the war, he said, were 'too late.' These words have dogged the Allies' every step.

'The Government has at last realized the stupendous blunder it committed'

ABOVE: British infantryman enjoy the modest spoils of war.
One is wearing a German greatcoat while another has attached
an eagle emblem to his helmet.

The Battle of Loos

In autumn 1915 the French commander, Field-Marshal Joseph Joffre, planned an offensive to drive the enemy off French soil. Despite the harsh experience of the spring, Joffre clung to the hope that throwing yet more men and weapons at the German lines might bring about his aim, but it failed.

In the advance, in Artois and Champagne, British troops did somewhat better. The First Army, commanded by Sir Douglas Haig, took Loos. This time it was the British forces who used gas, the first time they had done so. However, a lack of available reserves prevented the attack from being completely successful and the German forces were able to rally. The British reserves had been too far from the action, and Sir John French was blamed for this error of judgement. In December he was replaced by Field-Marshal Sir Douglas Haig as Commander in Chief of the British Expeditionary Force.

OPPOSITE INSET: Britain launched a major offensive to capture the Belgian town of Loos on September 25, 1915. The offensive marked the first occasion that the British used poison gas, but the gas was blown back towards the British lines in places, injuring at least 2,500 men. Haig abandoned the offensive after taking 50,000 casualties.

ABOVE: British soldiers returning from front-line duty at the Battle of Loos.

Verdun

Germany's plan for the new year involved a major fresh assault in the west. Falkenhayn, the German commander, believed that France could be defeated if his men launched an attack at the historic fort city of Verdun on the River Meuse. The general contended the city was so important to France's self-esteem and patriotism that the Allies would invest all their resources in defending it.

The offensive, 'Operation Gericht' (Judgement), was launched on February 21, 1916. 1,200 guns – including the huge and notorious 42-centimetre Big Bertha – launched what was to be one of the fiercest bombardments of the entire war.

Within four days the Germans had taken Fort Douaumont which was the largest of the city's famous defensive strongholds.

Pétain takes Command

Falkenhayn's trap was sprung and, as predicted, the French refused to cede a city that was a symbol of national pride, regardless of the fact that it was of no great strategic value. However, the French were not content merely to become cannon fodder for a hopeless cause. Under General Pétain, who assumed command of the city's defences, they determined to fight fire with fire. Pétain, the man who would later be reviled as a Nazi collaborator in World War II, became a national hero for the part he played in helping to save Verdun. Contrary to his later reputation, Pétain was a general of the modern school. He saw that the tradition of noble sacrifice – the usual French military response – had now to become subservient to modern technology, and his own artillery began inflicting heavy casualties on the German ranks.

Lines of communication were inevitably badly damaged, but Pétain ensured that one vital road to the south of the city remained open. This became known as the 'Voie Sacrée' or 'Sacred Way' and would be remembered for the ceaseless lines of trucks carrying fresh troops and supplies to the front. They also, of course, brought exhausted and shell-shocked men in the opposite direction for treatment, rest and recuperation. And the losses were heavy; the battle raged fiercely until June.

DAILY MAIL   FEBRUARY 29, 1916

The greatest battle

'The greatest battle of the greatest war' – for so the Germans already describe it – sways to and fro on the hills north of Verdun and seems steadily to extend. The Germans are attacking in enormous force and with the utmost fury. The incomparable French are maintaining the defence with that tenacious coolness and readiness to riposte which distinguish their modern army. There is as yet no sign of any decision and there is a good deal to suggest that the conflict is only in its first stage.

It has been suggested that the Germans are mad in attacking at one of the strongest points of the French line. The German staff, however, has every reason to be anxious to impress neutrals whose decision is believed to hang in the balance by dealing a terrific blow at the French. It has always held that any fortress and any position can be taken provided the necessary sacrifices are made.

The preliminary methods have been the same at Verdun as against the Russians on the Dunajetz – but with this immense difference, that at Verdun the French are well prepared, have numerous lines of defence behind their advanced positions, and are abundantly munitioned. Their most dangerous difficulties are that some new form of attack may be attempted by the enemy, whether by aircraft or by gas. The German bombardment is described as being of a fury which has never been approached before. That gives some measure of its violence. In the culminating point of Mackensen's assault on the Dunajetz 700,000 shells were discharged by the enemy in four hours, while, in addition, many new and devilish devices were employed in the shape of liquid fire, asphyxiating gas, and aircraft dropping asphyxiating bombs. The artillery fire in the present battle, we are told, is changing the very appearance of the country. But the monster guns are not this time all on Germany's side; the French are well equipped with rivals of the monster 17in. Kruppe.

OPPOSITE: French soldiers capture a German dug-out at Verdun. A German infantryman from the 242nd regiment lies dead in the foreground.

ABOVE: Casualties of Verdun. Around 700,000 men lost their lives in the campaign.

Battle of Jutland

Despite the passage of nearly two years of war, the British and German fleets had managed to avoid any full-scale confrontation. The British navy had more ships and greater fire power, even though Germany had made determined attempts to overtake them in the run-up to war. Britain's Royal Navy had not been used in battle since the days of Nelson a century earlier, and it was led by the cautious Admiral Sir John Jellicoe.

Jellicoe's fleet was based at Scapa Flow in the Orkney Islands, north of the Scottish mainland. Scapa Flow's position gave Britain a natural stranglehold on the North Sea and the German fleet had been confined to harbour for long periods, meaning the Central Powers were being slowly starved of resources. In January 1916, the new commander of Germany's High Seas Fleet, Admiral Reinhard Scheer, came up with a plan to neutralize Britain's naval superiority. He recognized that he had to attack, and formulated a plan to split up the enemy fleet and so increase his chance of victory. The Germans began to carry out raids on Britain's east coast, which forced Jellicoe to deploy a battle-cruiser squadron south from the Orkneys to Rosyth. This was exactly in accord with phase one of Scheer's scheme. His plan's second phase was to lure the battle-cruisers into the open sea by sailing a few German ships off the Norwegian coast. The British battle-cruiser squadron, led by Sir David Beatty, took the bait – and lying in wait for them, not far from the German outriders, was the entire High Seas Fleet. Everything seemed to be proceeding smoothly, but there was one serious flaw in their plans which was completely unknown to the Germans. British intelligence had cracked their naval code. Scheer had hoped to overpower Beatty's squadron of battle-cruisers and escape before the main British fleet could reach the scene but, thanks to the code-breakers, Jellicoe was already steaming into action.

BELOW: The British Fleet pictured shortly before war was declared.

OPPOSITE ABOVE: The two greatest naval forces in the world in battle in the North Sea off the Danish coast. Although German ships inflicted heavier losses, they suffered severely and did not risk a second engagement for the duration of the war.

OPPOSITE BELOW: Men gather on Fleet Street, the heart of London's newspaper industry, to read news of the latest sea battle.

Battle commences

Beatty's squadron engaged the German fleet at around 4.00 p.m. on May 31, 1916, and both HMS *Indefatigable* and *Queen Mary* exploded and sank within twenty minutes of each other. Out of *Indefatigable's* crew of 1,019 only two men survived, and 1,286 died on the Queen Mary.

By now, German gunnery was having the better of the exchange and Scheer was closing in fast, but he was still unaware of the approaching Grand Fleet. When Beatty sighted the main body of the German navy he turned his cruisers northwards towards Jellicoe and the main British fleet. It was now his turn to try and lure the enemy into a trap, and they duly followed. When the battle lines were finally drawn up it was Jellicoe who had a huge tactical advantage. By the time the two fleets engaged each other, his ships were arranged broadside across the German line, a manoeuvre known as 'crossing the T'. The Germans were coming under heavy bombardment and, despite the loss of HMS *Invincible* in yet another spectacular explosion, Jellicoe seemed certain of success.

Uncertain victory

In response, Scheer executed a brilliant 180-degree turn, his ships disappearing into the smoke and confusion. Jellicoe was reluctant to follow them, as always aware of the threat posed by torpedo fire, but he soon discovered that he didn't need to. For some reason, Scheer's forces performed another about-face manoeuvre and headed straight towards the British line. Jellicoe was in a dilemma. The Germans now had torpedoes within range – which could cause enormous losses – but engaging the enemy directly could bring an outright victory. He chose discretion and retreated, and by dawn the next morning the German fleet had slipped away. The battle was over.

Germany declared the Battle of Skaggerak, as they called Jutland, to be a great victory. There was some justification in this since Britain's losses were substantially higher. Fourteen British ships had been sunk, while Scheer had lost 11, and over 6,000 British sailors lost their lives while Germany's casualties were less than half that.

The Somme

The British now launched their own offensive on the Somme, with France playing a supporting role. An enormous week-long artillery bombardment began; it was a prelude to an attack by front-line soldiers which happened on July 1. Optimism was great among the British troops (as it had been among the Germans in February), and they sang: 'We beat 'em on the Marne, we beat 'em on the Aisne, we gave them hell at Neuve Chapelle and here we are again'. However, the artillery attack had not done its job properly. The Germans were heavily entrenched, and the bombardment proved to be ineffectual. Even worse, it also acted as a warning of the imminent assault. The Allied infantry left their trenches and moved across no man's land, attacking the German positions in close ranks. They were easy prey for the Germans' Maxim machine guns and by nightfall the casualty figure stood at about 57,000 – the worst losses on any one day in British military history. The French had been more tactically astute and made some gains, but overall it was a thoroughly bad day for the Allies.

BELOW: South African soldiers distinguished themselves in the battle for Delville Wood, renamed 'Devils Wood' by the Allies. At the height of the battle, German shells had rained down at a rate of 400 per minute, stripping the landscape bare.

The worst losses on any one day in British military history

DAILY MAIL   JULY 3, 1916

The first day's gains

A great battle had been fought. Another is being fought, and many more have yet to be fought. It will probably be called in England the Battle of Montauban and in France the Battle of the Somme. But, whatever we call it, or however we judge it, we must think of it as a battle of many battles, not to be likened in duration or extent, or perhaps intention, to such affairs as Neuve Chapelle or Loos.

It is and for many days will continue to be siege warfare, in which a small territorial gain may be a great strategical gain; and the price we must pay is to be judged by another measure than miles or furlongs or booty.

We are laying siege not to a place but to the German army – that great engine which had at last mounted to its final perfection and utter lust of dominion.

In the first battle, which I saw open with incredible artillery fury at 6 o'clock this morning, we have beaten the Germans by greater dash in the infantry and vastly superior weight in munitions. I may, perhaps, claim to be in some position to estimate methods and results. I watched the night bombardments, both German and British. I saw at close quarters the hurricane of the morning bombardment, which heralded that first gay, impetuous, and irresistible leap from the trenches, many of which I had visited earlier, knowing what was to come.

TOP: German casualties in a trench taken by the Allies, July 11, 1916.

ABOVE: Members of the Wiltshire Regiment rush on the Leipzig Salient, just south of Thiepval.

The Somme: Haig Miscalculates

Haig was undeterred by the losses. Although the casualty figures were never so bad again, the overall verdict on the Somme offensive was grim. The positions that Haig had hoped to secure on the very first day were still in German hands over four months later, in mid-November. The casualties on the Allied side exceeded 600,000, with German losses almost as bad at up to half a million.

BELOW: **30 June 1916, the calm before the storm. Two infantrymen share a quiet moment on the eve of the Somme offensive, which was to go down as the worst day in British military history.**

The Somme stripped bare

Left: The Somme battlefield after the offensive was launched. Haig's resolve remained unshaken despite the heavy casualties suffered in those first few days.

A concerned Lloyd George recalled Haig to London in early September. Once again the British Prime Minister felt unable to pull political rank over his senior military man.

1.75 million lives for little gain

RIGHT: On 15 December 1916, a month after the end of the Somme campaign, the Battle of Verdun also finally came to an end. Casualties for the two great battles of 1916 amounted to 1.75 million – and still there was deadlock. In both Britain and France there was friction between the military and political leaders, the latter determined that 1917 should not see losses on such a scale for so little gain.

BELOW: Men of the Royal Warwickshire Regiment take a well-earned rest out in the open during the Somme Campaign.

OPPOSITE ABOVE: Wounded men are lifted out of an ambulance wagon at a makeshift hospital station set up in an old farmhouse.

OPPOSITE BELOW: The barren landscape of the Somme battlefield.

German retreat

Withdrawals on the Western Front were central to Germany's new plan. As early as September 1916, work had begun on a new defensive line. It would shorten the front by about 30 miles and, as a consequence, provide a welcome reduction in the demand for resources. The German forces withdrew to the Siegfried Line (or the Hindenburg Line as the Allies called it) in the early months of 1917. A thousand square miles of land, which had been fought over so bitterly and which had cost so many casualties, was conceded almost at a stroke. But the withdrawal was not an unmitigated benefit for the Allies. As they retreated, the Germans adopted a comprehensive scorched-earth policy. The ground which they gave up would have no useful resources left – not even a drop of water, as all available supplies had been poisoned.

ABOVE: Troops from Australia and New Zealand patrol in Bapaume on March 29, 1917.

OPPOSITE: The German army left a trail of devastation in their wake. The Allies discover Bapaume ablaze as they enter the town on March 21, 1917.

DAILY MAIL   FEBRUARY 15, 1917

Sir D.Haig on his plans

'This year will be decisive in this sense: that we shall see the decision of the war on the fields of battle – that is to say, an event from which Germany will emerge beaten by force of arms.'

Speaking in French the purity and fluency of which surprised his visitors, the field-marshal, in answer to questions, said:

As to the next great offensive, it does not matter who makes the first move. If the enemy begins, whether it be in the north or the south, in salients which tempt him or on former battlefields, we are ready to receive him. His temerity will cost him dear. Our armies are well trained and in working order, so that the enemy's defeats will become a rout, depriving him at any moment of the possibility, even far behind his lines, of re-entrenching.

Shall we break through? Without the slightest doubt, with irresistible impulse and in many places. The German defence includes behind the lines a powerful system of railway lines. The first attacks in the great offensive may, therefore, at the beginning be limited. It has taken months and months to hold back this people of more than 50,000,000. It will take several more months yet to annihilate them. But we shall strike terribly and ceaselessly until we have accomplished the total destruction of their armies.

German forces adopt a scorched-earth policy as they withdraw to the Siegfried line

Nivelle's spring offensive

The Allies met to plan their own strategy for 1917 long before they became aware of the German withdrawal. This was essentially more of the same: concerted offensives on every front, with the aim of stretching the enemy forces to the limit. However, such a plan carried with it the prospect of another Somme – and that possibility haunted Lloyd George, who had become Prime Minister late in 1916. As it happened, a change in France's command structure dramatically changed the Allies' thinking, much to his relief. Joffre was replaced by General Robert Nivelle, in December. The new Commander in Chief of the French Army had distinguished himself at both the Battle of the Marne and Verdun. As a result his reputation was so good that he had little difficulty in bringing the political leaders with him – not least because he told them just what they wanted to hear. His scheme was for a joint Anglo–French spring offensive, on the Aisne. First would come saturation bombardment of the enemy positions, followed by a 'creeping barrage', behind which the infantry would advance. Nivelle predicted that a decisive breakthrough would come in only a few days. Haig did not agree – and nor did others – but Lloyd George's approval of the plan meant that his hands were effectively tied.

BELOW: A corner of the battlefield at Arras. The British launched the attack on April 9, 1917 as a diversionary operation in advance of Nivelle's main offensive on the Aisne.

OPPOSITE ABOVE: Soldiers pass through the ruins of Athies during the Battle of Arras.

OPPOSITE BELOW: British troops in Arras, June 7, 1917. The offensive cost the British 160,000 lives.

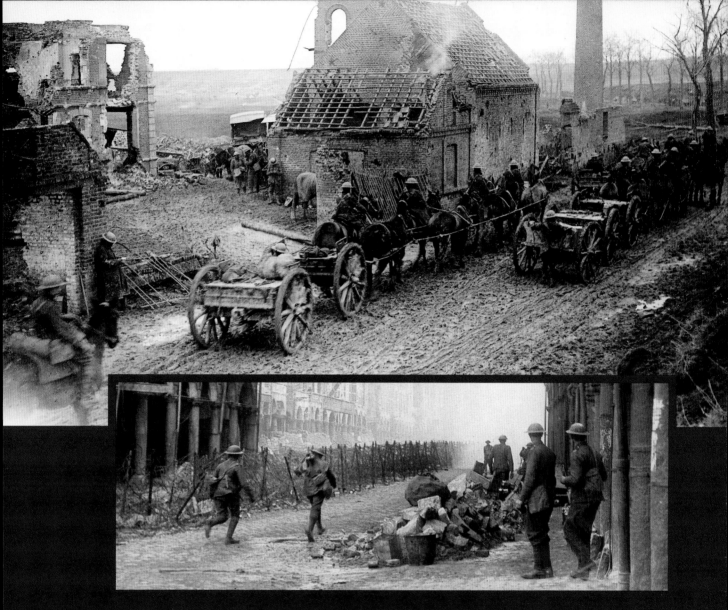

The British attack Arras

The offensive finally got underway on April 9, by which time it had already been undermined by Germany's withdrawal to the Hindenburg Line. Nivelle, though, pressed on. The Allies received early encouragement, as the Canadian Corps took Vimy Ridge and the British attacked Arras. But when the main thrust came, it proved to be yet another false hope, and the French army sustained over 100,000 casualties in the attack on Champagne. And, not surprisingly, the strict time limit that had been imposed fell by the wayside too. On May 15 Nivelle paid the price for his mistake: he was replaced by General Pétain. Popular though Pétain was, his appointment was not enough to assuage the emotions of the French infantry. After more failed promises and yet more mass slaughter they had had enough. There was mutiny on a massive scale.

Fortunately, the German Army was unaware of the situation, or they might have seized their chance. Pétain responded to the mutineers with a mixture of carrot and stick: the offensive was cancelled and attempts were made to improve the dire conditions on the front line. Anarchy could not go unpunished, however, and 23 mutineers faced a firing squad 'pour encourager les autres'.

The Battle of Vimy Ridge

BELOW: The Battle of Vimy Ridge, April 1917. Germans surrendering to the Canadians during the taking of the ridge. The battle, which took place from 9 to 12 April 1917, was part of the opening phase of the British-led Battle of Arras, a diversionary attack for the French Nivelle Offensive.

Passchendaele

Following Nivelle's disastrous spring offensive, the French were in no position to instigate another attack on the Western Front. Haig, however, was determined to do so; his authority had been restored by the failure of Nivelle's offensive, which he had opposed. His idea was to break through the German line at Ypres and then push through to the Belgian coast, severing the enemy's right flank. Such a plan also meant that the Allies would be within striking distance of the German U-boat bases at Ostend and Zeebrugge. All the Entente Powers were still deeply concerned by Germany's U-boat policy and any action which might harm their submarines was therefore a tempting one. Pétain was sceptical, favouring a defensive operation until the US could mobilize in significant numbers, and Lloyd George was still concerned about the possibility of another Somme. But the United States was a long way from being ready, and there were still weaknesses in the French army. Haig saw the chance of Britain gaining a glorious victory. He got his wish and his plans for the third Battle of Ypres – or Passchendaele, as it would come to be known – got under way.

BELOW: A wounded soldier receives a welcome helping hand. The events of 1916 would lead many front-line troops to question the cause they were fighting for, though the camaraderie remained unshakeable.

OPPOSITE: A Belgian woman sells oranges to British troops as they head to the front in Flanders.

Haig saw the chance of Britain gaining a glorious victory.

The battle for Messines Ridge

Haig's first target was the Messines Ridge south of Ypres which was a key vantage point; the Germans had held it for two years. On June 7, General Sir Herbert Plumer led a successful attack on the ridge. From then on preparations for the main assault could continue unobserved and unhindered by targeted enemy action. However, these preparations took six weeks – time which the Germans put to good use.

BELOW: The war causes congestion in Fricourt, France, August 8, 1917.

DAILY MAIL   JUNE 8, 1917

Haig strikes

We attacked at 3.10 a.m. the German positions on the Messines-Wytschaete Ridge [south of Ypres] on a front of over 9 miles. We have everywhere captured our first objectives, and further progress is reported to be satisfactory along the whole front of attack.

The Battle of Messines Ridge, as the sequel to the Battle of Vimy Ridge, will be almost the greatest battle in our history, if we keep what we have won. At the moment that I write our skied observers see German divisions in mass gathering for attack, but whatever may happen in the future it remains that we took what we meant to take exactly as we meant to take it and at the precise minute we meant to take it.

Rain and mud at Passchendaele

The rain came earlier than usual and was especially heavy. Haig had planned massive bombardment to signal the start of the main assault on Passchendaele, but the shells broke up muddy ground whose drainage system had collapsed in the deluge. The advancing British soldiers had to contend with thick sticky mud and water-filled craters as well as enemy fire, but the Germans were not in the same position. They had abandoned the idea of trying to keep to entrenched positions in such appalling conditions, and defended their lines with machine guns housed in pillboxes instead.

It took another month before the weather improved and the Allies finally gained a glimpse of Passchendaele Ridge, which had been one of the first-day objectives. The rain returned in October but Haig remained unwavering in his aim. He was convinced that the German army was about to crack and was consumed by the need to capture Passchendaele itself. Passchendaele was eventually taken on November 2, though at enormous cost. The line had only advanced five miles, but more than 250,000 casualties had been sustained for that short distance. Haig's plans were a complete failure. The ports of Zeebrugge and Ostend continued to maintain the U-boats that had been inflicting terrible losses on Allied shipping, and the German army was far from surrendering.

ABOVE: Soldiers shelter in the flooded shell holes of the Passchendaele battlefield.

OPPOSITE: British casualties mounted to almost 250,000 during the battle for Passchendaele. Here the wounded lie in open fields awaiting treatment.

Swamp of death and pain

Every inch we gained in Friday's battle is worth a mile as common distance is reckoned. Some troops went forward 1,700 yards or even more, fighting all the way; and when their relic came back some part of that heroic journey no enemy dared follow them, so foul and cruel was their track.

They left behind them a Golgotha, a no man's land, a dead man's land. Five or six miles separate our troops from any place where you can step firm, where you can find any break in the swamp. It is a nightmare journey to traverse it, in spite of the ceaseless labour of pioneers.

Our soldiers coming out of this swamp of death and pain maintain incredible serenity. If we could advance so far in such conditions we could go anywhere in fine weather. We were nowhere beaten by the enemy, though more defensive wire was left round shell-holes and pill-boxes and fewer machine gunners knocked out than in any recent attack. We were beaten by the rain that began to fall in torrents at midnight before the attack, so they all say and feel, and so it was.

One of them, still full of humour, said he considered Friday an unlucky day for him. 'You see,' he argued, 'I was first hit in the shoulder by a machine-gun bullet, and as I stumbled was hit in the foot, and as I lay another hit me in the foot and another hit me in the side. Decidedly Friday is an unlucky day.' It was a terrible day for wounded men, and alternate advance and retreat now always leave a wide, indeterminable no man's land from which escape to the mercy of either side is hard. But the best is being done, and the immortal heroism of the stretcher-bearers was backed by both the daring and skilful work of doctors at advance dressing stations and ambulance drivers a little farther back.

The trouble was how to find people or places. Wounded men, runners, contact officers, and even whole platoons had amazing journeys among shells and bullets searching for dressing-station headquarters, objective or what not, and, as we know, even Germans on the pure defensive had similar trouble and their units were inextricably confused. It was all due, as one of them said, to the sump, or morass.

All that can be said of the battle is that we are a little higher up the slope than we were and a little further along the crest road to Passchendaele. How we succeeded in capturing over 700 prisoners is one of the marvels of the day. A marvel, too, is the pile of German machine guns. They are some small concrete proof of the superhuman efforts of our infantry. If the world has supermen they were the men who waded forward up to their hips astride the Ravelbeck and stormed concrete and iron with flesh and blood. They were at least the peers of the men who fought 'upon their stumps' at Chevy Chase.

To-day the artillery fire has died down, the sun is bright, though the cold west wind threatens showers.

The Battle of Cambrai

To maintain momentum after Passchendaele, the Allies launched a last offensive for the year on the Western Front. At the Battle of Cambrai, which opened on November 20, over 400 tanks were deployed, spearheading the attack. This was the first time tanks had been seen on a battlefield in such numbers. There were some encouraging early gains, but a combination of direct hits and mechanical breakdowns meant that tank numbers were severely reduced after the initial breakthrough. In the end, the German Army counterattacked and the usual stalemate was restored.

Mixed review for the Allies

1917 had been a year fraught with difficulties for the Allies, but it ended on a rather brighter note as news came through that Field Marshal Allenby's Egyptian Expeditionary Force had marched into Jerusalem on December 9, capturing Beersheba and Gaza on the way. There was little reason for celebration on the other main fronts on land. There was a complete collapse in the east following the Russian Revolution; there had been the fiasco of Nivelle's spring offensive and Passchendaele in the west, and defeat at Caporetto in Italy. However, the German U-boat war, which had been devastating to the Allies in the early months of the year, had moderated somewhat. The Allies had been using a convoy system, with merchant ships travelling together under the protection of warships, and this had helped to improve survival rates. Even so, rationing had to be introduced in Britain at the end of the year, and even the royal family succumbed to it. Germany's attempt to bring Britain to her knees had, ultimately, failed. And 1918 might be much better – there was the prospect of the American Expeditionary Force led by General John Pershing becoming a key part of the effort on the Western Front. Their recruits and conscripts were completing their training and becoming ready for frontline duty.

BELOW: British Infantry dodge machine gun fire near Cambrai. The Allies soon became victims of their own success; the tanks, which had been vital to the spectacular gains on the first day, pushed on too far ahead of the troops, allowing for an easy German counterattack.

OPPOSITE BELOW: The East Anglian division occupies a German trench on the first day of the Battle of Cambrai.

OPPOSITE ABOVE: Medics rush to pull a wounded man off the battlefield. Thousands of medics lost their lives during the war as they tried to rescue the wounded.

Over 400 tanks were deployed, spearheading the attack

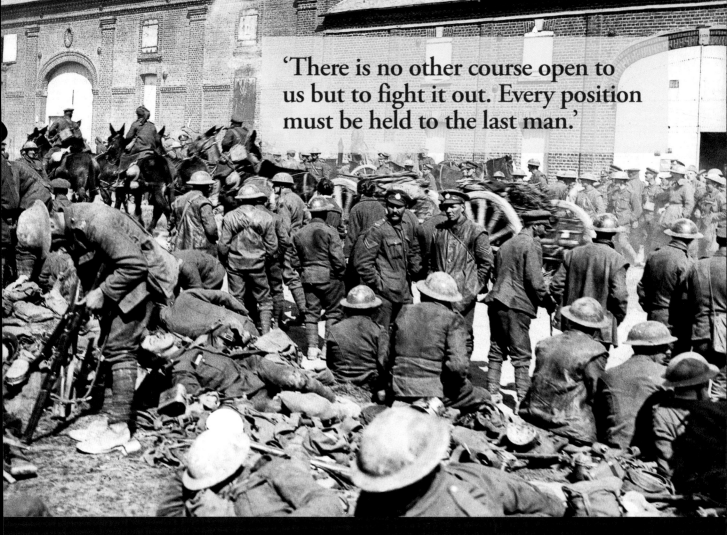

'There is no other course open to us but to fight it out. Every position must be held to the last man.'

Ludendorff's offensives

Marshal Ferdinand Foch became the de facto Supreme Allied Commander of the Western Front on March 26. He had the immediate problem of pulling together the Allied defences and stopping the potentially disastrous German advance. The town of Amiens, Foch quickly realized, would be an immediate target for the enemy and he decided that it must be defended at all costs. In this he was helped, paradoxically, by the Germans and specifically by Ludendorff, who decided to advance on a wide front instead of concentrating his efforts on taking Amiens itself. As the days passed, the Allied line became much stronger and better reinforced, while the German line was getting overstretched and weaker. The German advance finally petered out on April 8. It had lost its vital momentum.

Ludendorff decided to change the point of attack in the hope of revitalizing the attack. A fresh offensive was launched around the River Lys to the north, which had originally been considered as an alternative to Operation Michael. It now became the focus of a secondary onslaught, and once again there was an immediate breakthrough which offered encouragement to the Germans. Haig issued a Special Order of the Day on April 11. This was, in effect, a rallying call to all the ranks: 'There is no other course open to us but to fight it out. Every position must be held to the last man; there must be no retirement. There is no other course open to us but to fight it out.'

Second Battle of Marne

The final stages had to be played out on the Western Front. Ludendorff tried yet another initiative on May 27, this time against the French Sixth Army along the Chemin des Dames. The German army swept across the Aisne and reached the Marne. This suddenly threatened Paris, which was only some 50 miles away, and there was a partial evacuation of the city. Paris did come under fire from the German guns, but the attack was halted. The German army had made great territorial gains and inflicted considerable losses on the Allies in three short months of concerted effort. However, more and more American divisions were arriving, and the Allied losses were not as critical as those sustained by Ludendorff. In a single month – June – his army suffered over 200,000 casualties. June also saw the arrival of the flu epidemic in the German ranks, diminishing their strength even further.

On July 15, Ludendorff made a final effort to achieve a breakthrough. There was an offensive around Rheims. Three days later the French, who were supported by fresh American troops, counter-attacked. This became known as the Second Battle of the Marne, and proved to be the turning point. From this time on, right until the end of hostilities in November, Germany would be on the retreat.

The Battle of Amiens

The Allies were now forcing Ludendorff's army backwards relentlessly. The morale of the rival forces changed accordingly – and the poor situation of the German forces did not improve. The Battle of Amiens took place on August 8, with General Rawlinson leading a combined Allied force. They caught the Germans completely off-guard and quickly shattered any remaining hopes of victory which they might have had. Over 2,000 guns bombarded the German line and about 400 tanks were deployed to support the infantry as they advanced.

Allied air supremacy

The Allies now had massive air supremacy, partly due to the RAF, which had recently been formed. Reconnaissance aircraft had improved, and information about enemy positions and batteries could now be relayed much more efficiently. The backroom staff had also finally come up with a solution to the problem of synchronizing machine-gun fire with the rotation of the propellers, some three years after Anthony Fokker had achieved the same thing for the Germans. The rate of attrition among the flyers was high, however: on the first day of the Amiens offensive the RAF lost 45 planes to anti-aircraft fire. Despite this, their contribution to the Allies' ultimate success was significant.

The Amiens offensive was undoubtedly disastrous for the Central Powers, and Ludendorff declared it to be 'the black day of the German army'. The final blow would be for the Allies to breach the Germans' Siegfried Line, and this finally happened on September 29. Even before that, both Ludendorff and the Kaiser knew that the outcome was now set. The only thing left was to bring the war to an end.

Over 2,000 guns bombarded the German line and about 400 tanks were deployed

Armistice

ABOVE: British soldiers in the trenches on the outskirts of Thiepval, September 5, 1918.

OPPOSITE: Refreshments for the wounded during the British advance in the west.

On November 8, Marshal Foch received an armistice delegation from Germany in a railway carriage in the forest of Compiegne. The Germans were given seventy-two hours to agree to the terms laid down, which included the introduction of democracy to the country, but the delegates didn't need that much time. The following day Kaiser Wilhelm abdicated, leaving for neutral Holland. The armistice was signed at 5.00 in the morning on November 11, and was to come into force six hours later, at 11 a.m. There was some fighting until the very last minute.

LANCELLE, BOTTIER

ABOVE: Searching the recently bombed streets
following the German withdrawal.

This is a Transatlantic Press Book
First published in 2012

Transatlantic Press
38 Copthorne Road, Croxley Green, Hertfordshire, UK

© Atlantic Publishing

Photographs © Associated Newspapers Archive

A catalogue record for this book is available from the British Library.